Life After Leaping In

Change Management in a Changing World

Abi Potter Clough

Westshore Press

Westshore Press
Tampa, FL United States

www.LifeAfterLeapingIn.com

Copyright © 2021 Abi Potter Clough
All rights reserved.

Abi Potter Clough reserves the moral right to be identified as the author of this work.

ISBN: 978-1-7367580-3-8

To Mark. You inspire me.

Part One

Beginning

Chapter 1 – Why Leap?

In 2013, Sheryl Sandberg's famous pithy advice to women to "lean in" made the rounds in corporate America. Organizations created networking groups featuring the concept to give women a place to share stories and to learn from each other. She encouraged women to lean in at the workplace to get ahead.

I took this advice and sprinted off with it. I always wanted to be different, to stand out, and so, while leaning in sounded great, I decided to *leap* in with everything I had. Excelling at work became part of my identity. If I'm being perfectly honest, at times it *was* my identity.

Throwing myself in headfirst, leaping in with everything I can, has been my way of living for as long as I can recall. From my all-consuming passion for horses, devoting myself to learning Spanish in high school and college, finishing my course studies quickly to become the first person at my office to earn a prestigious insurance designation, and traveling to China and Switzerland as part of my MBA studies, I give myself entirely to my current passion.

My job was no different. I volunteered for Saturday shifts and catastrophe duty, taught (and took) insurance classes, volunteered for community events like Habitat for Humanity and Relay for Life with work friends, and promoted the company every chance I had. I loved our mission, our values, and Snoopy.

Earning my CPCU – which stands for Chartered Property Casualty Underwriter – changed my life in a number of ways, and not all of them professional.

My best friends are CPCUs, I dated a CPCU for a while, and my travel was vacations added to CPCU and other risk management conferences. I structured my travel purposefully and went to events and meetings in London, Amsterdam, Bermuda, Singapore, and Zurich, as well as some beautiful US destinations – New Orleans, San Diego, and Phoenix were my favorites.

Life was good! And it was immersive. I threw myself into everything I did.

I also spent time developing my social media presence and my personal brand, and those reflected my passion for the risk management and insurance industry, as well as my fun passions: travel, horses, dogs, food. I was sharing myself and leaping in a little more with every social media post.

For me, leaping in is a lifelong habit. I have learned it doesn't suit everyone, though. Sometimes people want to suppress this tendency when they see it in others. But I've learned to ignore this and embrace my natural leaps – being passionate and purposeful in how I live my life.

Here's how I did it.

It was the end of September, a gorgeous autumn morning in upstate New York when the air is brisk but not yet cold, the leaves are colorful, and the horses are fresh. Winter remains a distant worry and there still will be some random 70-degree, sun-drenched afternoons that will feel like heaven. But this morning is bright and crisp, and the coffee is hot, and I've recently returned from one of my favorite places to visit.

I'd been in New Orleans for a CPCU conference and always leave on a complete high after seeing my best friends, meeting new people, hosting networking events, and presenting with amazing colleagues to engaged audiences. Plus, all the fun of the Crescent City!

My two best friends and I shared beignets and coffee at Café Du Monde, and I got a little too happy one night drinking hurricanes at Pat O'Brien's. It was the kind of happy where your besties hop in an Uber with you and take you back to the hotel to eat French fries and chat like schoolgirls instead of taking the walking ghost tour of the city; the kind of happy where you text 'I love you' to your new boyfriend for the first time with absolute joy and abandon because you feel it so intensely; the kind of happy where every stranger is a friend and the city lights put a shine on everything.

I came back to New York refreshed and with new ideas for challenges I'd been facing at work. I was excited to share things I had learned with my team so I powered up my laptop early on that Thursday morning.

It was 9:26 a.m. on September 26 when my boss pinged me and asked if I had a minute. That was about all the time I had before my first meeting of the day but I was excited to connect with her and catch up. She called me and then she said my director was on the line as well.

I'm an optimist by nature and I had applied for a promotion before I left for New Orleans, so I thought this phone call might be welcomed news. That is, until my director told me it wasn't a friendly call after all.

My heart pounding, I listened to her lay me off. I muted my phone as she read the rather long canned speech about economics, the company's results, and the next steps. Sometimes there is so much emotion at once that there comes a point when your physiological response overwhelms you, and you can't think or speak.

My heart thumping in my chest was the only sound I heard. The blood rushing through my head left me weak-kneed, and I could not have responded even if I wanted to. It was a terrifying feeling, this dread and grief and shock I experienced viscerally throughout my body.

I remember thanking her but not much else. This was Thursday morning, and she gave me the rest of the day and Friday off. After that I'd be expected to finish the next month at my job to wrap things up and train someone else on my projects.

When the call ended, I stood staring out the window at the For Sale sign hanging in my yard, my dreams hanging tenuously in the cool morning air along with it.

Do I take the house off the market and stay in New York? Is it time to play it safe? Or do I leap into this relocation and try to make the move even after my layoff?

One thing I knew for sure was that I did not ever want to feel the way I did when I was on the call hearing this news. My heart was pounding through my body, overwhelming my senses and my thoughts. I resolved to never give that control to another person again. Whatever happened in my future, it had to be different. I had to be in control.

This was about the time I stopped sleeping. I could usually fall asleep with no problem, but after a few hours of restless sleep I was wide awake. At 2 a.m., wake to pee. At 2:30 still up; 3 a.m. eyes wide open; 4 a.m. so tired but so awake; 5 a.m. give up and get up. Sometimes I would read in bed, sometimes I would cry in the dark, and at other times I got up and cleaned or organized something.

Why do I leap

Growing up, I never thought I was good enough. Competitive by both nature and nurture, my drive to succeed and to be the best was often isolating. I was confident I could do anything, though, and that has stuck with me while I've learned to manage my competitive nature.

I used to describe myself as Type A, and that could still be an accurate if somewhat limiting description of me. I like to win but now I love to find ways we can all win, instead of winning at the expense of others.

Having a strong network of great female friends has helped me understand how promoting and amplifying others is one of the best things I can do and has quelled my "win-at-all-cost" tendencies. My girlfriends have made me better.

I am passionate about things I love and can fall into all-consuming bliss when I find a new passion. When I was a child, all I wanted to do was ride horses. My parents eventually caved and started me on riding lessons and that was it, I was hooked – the sight, sound, feel, and smell of horses was everything.

Still is.

Even today, at the barn and in the saddle are where I'm most comfortable. Escaping to the barn and burying my face in my horse's mane was my therapy. Galloping across a field, flying over jumps, and racing through trails I threw off my insecurities and thrived.

I grew up in horse barns around New York; being a working student, having horses, training, teaching, riding, competing, and immersing myself in that world. My early horses – Moon, Magic, and Avanti – are still some of my best teachers and I count myself extraordinarily lucky to have had them in my life.

Moon taught me patience; Magic taught me kindness; and Avanti taught me there are times when incredible beauty, talent, and luck combine, and that life is amazing.

I remember winning my first blue ribbon at a horse show at Southlands in Rhinebeck, NY. I was mounted on the sweetest little grey pony, Paris – a round little thing who spent her life dutifully taking care of little children.

A saint with fur and hooves.

It's funny because some ponies are fuzzy little angels who stop the moment their tiny riders lose their balance and stand gingerly waiting patiently while a child rebalances awkwardly in the saddle.

And other ponies, well, they're the ones that make us better riders. The ones that like to pretend all is well as they trot placidly around the ring but then suddenly, BAM! They stop and pull the reins through their tiny rider's hands and drop their noses to the ground, resulting in the child catapulting over the pony's head. Thank goodness for helmets and cartilage.

But Paris, she was the angelic kind. She sported me around the ring as I put her through her careful paces. We may have trotted over some tiny crossrails, too. I recall lining up in the middle of the ring after the class in an uneven line with the other kids and their mounts to listen to the judge. I was too young to care about results or to really understand anything at that moment other than how happy I felt to be riding and how beautiful I thought Paris was.

Suddenly, though, the judge went through the results and my number was called last, meaning we came in first!

It was so exciting!

The judge pinned the blue ribbon on Paris' bridle, and I beamed like we had won the Kentucky Derby. The crowd went wild and I was thrilled! My mom took a picture of us after we left the ring and I treasured that picture for years – I was sitting so proudly on Paris, the bright blue ribbon laying on her white mane, her neck elegantly arched.

Someone came up to congratulate me, and I remember my mother saying she was so surprised I won that "you could have pushed me over with a feather." Now, I was little, six or seven at this point, and I had never heard that expression before.

I kept smiling but my smile cracked a little. What did she mean? Why was she so surprised I had won? Didn't I deserve to win?

Looking back, I have spent years trying to overcome that feeling and to believe I am good enough. Leaping in, wanting to learn quickly and be good at new things, and avoiding things I am bad at became my pattern. I didn't like the uncomfortable feeling that comes from not knowing how to do something.

Asking for help meant admitting I didn't know something, and that was never safe to me. Being vulnerable was not encouraged and so I wouldn't act vulnerable. I understand now this was not a flaw of my parents, but rather a strength they thought they were imparting.

There is a certain peace that comes from leaping in, as well. If I leap in and find an all-consuming passion to focus my energy, that means less time for anxiety to creep in and take over. Too much time to think can be my downfall – overthinking paralyzes me from taking forward movement. One step at a time and all, but when you are overwhelmed with doubts even one step can be a near-impossible challenge. I learned for me, though, throwing myself into my passions can be cathartic.

When I first started my career in insurance and was hired as a claims adjuster, I had no idea what the job would entail. I remember telling my mom I got the job and she asked what an adjuster adjusted, and I said I had no idea, but I would learn!

did learn and the more I knew, the more I loved. The job became a passion for me, and I threw myself into learning everything I could about insurance and risk management. Being young, female, and freshly out of college, I wanted to prove myself.

I took classes and studied for exams to earn designations and licenses. Earning my CPCU was one of my proudest accomplishments. Working in claims is where you help people and fulfill the promise the insurance company made to the policyholder when the policy was purchased, and I loved helping people during challenging times.

I handled overflow calls during Superstorm Sandy when we were inundated with customers needing help. On those calls, it was my job to talk to customers who were first reporting their damages from the storm. It was life-changing for me. I loved my job and was proud to be a part of a company doing great work to help people.

When I lost my job, I lost part of my identity.

Fifteen years were gone in a five-minute phone call. The whole of my adult life I had been Abi at MetLife. Now I was just Abi, and frankly I was not sure who that was without my usual identifiers.

Who was she?

Was *Just Abi* good enough?

I had spent 15 years creating this identity – Abi/MetLife/New York. Was I good enough without those descriptors?

Chapter 2 – Loyalty

Loyalty is a funny concept. I was raised to believe in loyalty, stability, and doing the "right thing." My sheltered thinking was very black and white, as perhaps it is for many children raised in small towns. My grandparents were born into the Great Depression. I remember my grandmother drying and reusing paper towels, and her leftovers were stored in old Cool Whip and margarine containers. She had the blue Danish butter cookie tin filled with buttons and sundry sewing supplies, the ubiquitous red tomato pin cushion topping off the lot.

My parents raised me to look for stability, to believe in loyalty to an employer. My goal was full pension retirement. They sought out a stable life, and then passed to me this value. Tenure was their dream; they wanted my sister and me to be teachers with (what they hoped would be) secure jobs and stable futures. Spoiler alert, neither of us are teachers – but we are both happy!

There is nothing quite like the generational fears passed down to children as realities to overcome, though. To learn that the way you have always thought is not the way you always will think is an incredible realization. The world works in many ways, not only the one we were taught as children.

The question of stability or adventure has been a driving force for me. Steady and secure employment meant, to me, a 9-to-5 career: an office job with dark suits, Louboutin shoes, and a corner office with tall windows. I loved working for a global company with name-brand recognition and my dream seemed to be coming true.

As the years passed, though, I realized employment was no longer a warm fuzzy relationship between worker and company, if it ever was. Rather, it was transactional; if I was the best fit at the right time for the right price, I could stay.

But being the "best fit" didn't mean I was the best person at my job. It meant that financially, I best fit the algorithm assigned to the work being done. Sure, I was good at my job and I performed well, but once the financial fit was no longer a match, the algorithm shifted me to the layoff list.

At my company, layoff cycles typically happened in the fall and bonus and raise cycles were in the springtime. The last year I was there, I had a great spring, and I paid for it in the fall.

My old thinking was loyalty to a company. My new thinking is loyalty to myself. It may not look quite the same as my childhood 9 to 5 dream, but my search for adventure over stability continues. Gig work is the new economy, and many people are making money in different ways. The internet allows the freedom to find work in new ways and gig work is gaining momentum and respectability.

My parent's generation may have considered gig work to be less respectful than a full-time job. It was difficult getting over that stigma of what I was raised to think I should do and want. It was embarrassing to consider I had failed at a full-time job and I worried it was lazy to spend my time writing and reading, looking for more meaning to my days than I had when working my typical nine-hour workday.

But giving my all to a company and hoping they were loyal back seemed like a losing proposition when it is all about the bottom-line finances. When it came down to it, there was no individual person making the decision to lay me off. The algorithm did the work, and loyalty is not a factor in the equation.

That was a harsh reality to face, learning that my expectations were false. I learned what I should expect is simply today; an at-will employment contract that can end tomorrow. It is not personal, and the relationship should in fact end when it no longer makes sense for both parties.

I was briefly married; a twentysomething mistake fueled by childish expectations of what my life should look like. I watched my sweet father-in-law retire from his 37-year career with the same company, an amazing accomplishment by many standards. I was not yet 37 myself, and it affected me significantly to think of working at one place my entire life. It seemed stifling and limiting. My young mind craved more new experiences, and having barely started my career, I knew I would not last 37 years at one employer.

Having a sense of loyalty to my employer, even though it was misplaced, had given me a certain set of expectations of behavior. On a basic level, I thought that because we were loyal to each other

I could predict their actions, what my days would entail, and how my reviews would go. Trusting them meant I could trust their words and predict future actions. But this is where loyalty to a company can become problematic.

Some philosophers go a step further and argue loyalty can only be to another individual, and that one aspect of loyalty is that it is expected to be returned. But is that a realistic expectation from an individual to have of a company?

If a person is loyal to a company, in this case defined by staying at the company, doing a good job, and promoting the business in public, should they expect loyalty in return as they might in a personal relationship with another individual?

The lines are even fuzzier because employees are human and develop relationships with each other. It can feel a bit like being loyal to an individual as well as the company, particularly when you are close with colleagues.

Your boss is not your friend, though, even though it may feel that way when you are working long hours together to achieve challenging goals and believing in the same things. It is a false expectation to think your boss will be able to defend you or save your job. Even if they wanted to, they might not have the power or want to invest the goodwill needed to do so.

There was also this persistent feeling throughout my career that trying harder was the way to get ahead, pushing harder, leaping in further, by working longer hours, checking email at nights and on the weekends, avoiding vacations or bringing my laptop with me.

This habit once led to a fight at a beach house with an ex-boyfriend who became salty that I was checking email while we were traveling. But I was up for a promotion and had to be available even while vacationing...or so I thought.

I leaped in further when things were tough and this strategy worked for a while. I equated leaping in with being loyal. All this, plus being seen at company events, being vocal about supporting the company in public, and generally flying the company flag seemed the right way to behave in return for their loyalty in employing me.

Changing my thinking around loyalty to a company was an important growth moment for me. Really, it was a little mind-blowing. The idea that I was strictly a number to the company turned out to be very freeing, but I did take it personally at times in the beginning and had to work through that.

There were a lot of reasons they should want to keep me, both anecdotal and metric-based, and in the end, I had to let go of all of that. I realized I had become stagnant, and fear kept me at my job. I began to look at the layoff like an opportunity for greatness, not a betrayal of trust.

I gained so much from my 15-year career there, and I know I made a difference in a variety of ways between the people I mentored and taught, programs I created, and customers I helped.

That is what I learned to take from the experience, along with the knowledge that leaping in is a great thing if I remember to remain loyal to myself along the way.

Chapter 3 – Why Change?

There is comfort in familiarity, and sometimes, comfort is an anchor. I grew up in the Hudson Valley of New York, in a little village nestled in the valley formed by the Hudson River and the Catskill Mountains. My hometown is a fairytale place and I loved growing up there. My love for Rhinebeck is one reason I stayed in New York State for as long as I did. Life was predictable. The seasons would change as they always had, and New York enjoys an even mix of all four seasons.

I moved further north in New York state for my undergraduate program and settled outside of the state capital in a small suburb called Rotterdam. Toward the end of my time there, winter seemed to last longer and longer, stealing more than its fair share of the year's weather.

As a child, the end of spring marked the beginning of long, lazy summer days, and the start of colder nights meant back to school and the return of jackets, jeans, and frosty mornings. Christmas and New Year's Eve broke up the harsh winter months only to start my longing for warmer days until spring came. Very cyclical and very predictable.

My life rotated around these annual weather changes, between studying, sports schedules, and horse shows in the fair months. As an adult, I realized I fell into the same way of thinking. Patterns dictated by weather dictated by time of year.

Day after day
month after month
year after year.

It began to feel oppressive when I realized my life could be the same in one, five-, or ten-years' time.

I could be living in my house, working at the same place, driving the same car, going to the barn. Sure, there would be adventures and exciting things to brighten the days and to look forward to: a trip to a new place, a visit to see friends in NYC, maybe a frivolous purchase to consider. But the daily reality, the bulk of my life, was going to be the same. This was a lifelong pattern for me, having lived in the same area and following the changing seasons as a kind of hourglass for my life.

I lived in my house for 15 years, which seemingly passed in an instant, as these things often do. When I bought my house, I was young and looking for my version of the American dream. I wanted marriage, a house with a yard and dogs, suburban living. The things I was conditioned to want from a young age and took comfort in having. It felt natural to work toward these goals and at first, living that life, I loved that stability very much.

My little blue house at the end of the street with a big yard was perfect for me. I got married and we adopted two retired racing greyhounds who fit the lazy aesthetic of our home quite nicely. Eddie and Mollie were tall, sweet, goofy pups who had spent their early years racing and their later years sleeping on my couch.

But like summer fading into winter, things kept changing. My marriage ended and I went to grad school, but still I lived in my little blue house with my hounds and sweet black cat.

It was funny how easily I settled into living alone. When my ex moved out, the peacefulness of a quiet home was addicting. I wholly loved living by myself, with the dogs and cat, no TV, no constant noise. I could focus on school, work, and myself, and I did.

It was freeing. At first.

Over time, I dated, had relationships, made friends, and was more comfortable in my place and with myself. I got too comfortable, though, and stopped challenging myself. It was easy to stay home, and even more so when the weather was rough.

Cold, windy winters kept me inside and the deep winter darkness isolated me further. It was hard to force myself outside and the walls were closing in during the long winters. Rotterdam averages a mere 180 sunny days per year and as the years passed, I dreaded every one of the remaining 185 dreary, grey days. I needed the scales to tip in the other direction.

Over the last few years that I lived in New York, this dichotomy inside me grew deeper. I loved New York and have a strong connection to the places I grew up. Taking the train to Manhattan was one of my favorite things to do. The tracks follow the Hudson River south from Albany meandering through my homeland, passing green fields that sloped gently to the river's edge where I rode horses when I was young.

The familiar station stop in Rhinecliff haunted me every time the train passed through; it used to be a rambling run-down hotel where as teens we made our first clumsy attempts at being adults. The bar was loud and smoky, the floor sticky and air stale. It stood, ramshackle, rising above the train tracks next to the river.

In my memories it is always dark, grey, and loud there. The cacophony of teen voices, a bad house band, and the occasional train passing a few steps beyond the crumbling patio was constant.

The Hotel changed me when we were 16 and suffered an immeasurable tragedy there – the violent death of a classmate ripping away remaining remnants of childhood and shoving us into young adulthood.

The Hotel is now turned into an expensive bespoke bed and breakfast. Our teen hangout became an elegant wedding venue and weekend escape from Manhattan, echoing the transition of many places in Rhinebeck. It is still an incredible town, the place I dream of on restless nights, but it represents old patterns to me.

I had to leave to change.

There is a Rush song about having freewill that a college boyfriend of mine loved; I remember him singing it at the poolhall where we hung out playing darts and drinking beer when wide-eyed optimism and excitement were our norm. The lyrics are talk about how not deciding is still making a choice. This 40-year-old quote perfectly describes me when I realized I needed to make a major life change.

I was passively living my life, going day to day, letting the seasons and flow of life control me. I was not actively deciding the direction of my life. This was not who I was, but to be honest, I know longer knew who I was.

Ducky

There was another reason I had to leave New York and was struggling to make a big change. As I was nearing the end of grad school, I knew I needed a hobby to fill the extra time I was looking forward to having and decided to find a barn and get back in the saddle.

I had taken a few years without riding while working and saving money, and now was in a place where I could ride again. It was amazing to go back as an adult after a few years off! I found an incredible barn in New York that became my second home.

It was at HillCroft that I met Ducky. A 17.1-hand grey Trakehner, she was stunning and everything I wanted in a mount. She was complicated as many mares are, and highly intelligent. Kind, goofy, and sensitive, her soulful brown eyes spoke volumes. Everyone who enjoys a hobby has their perfect thing; if you play guitar there is that one fantasy guitar you want. Golfers want their dream set of clubs, and car enthusiasts have their eyes on a perfect model year.

For me, Ducky was my perfect horse. She was never easy, and I never wanted easy. She did not love everyone, so earning her trust and admiration was special. We developed a bond I have never had with another horse. I have worked with lots of horses in my life, and she was utterly unique. We met at the right time; I could not have handled a sensitive ride like her when I was younger.

When I first met her, she was a different horse. She was a challenge on the ground, often pinning her ears, threatening to bite or kick, and moving her body into you to intimidate and control the situation. She was constantly moving and would take off back to her stall when I took her off the crossties to bridle her.

She would strike out with a hoof when you went to tighten the girth or twist back to try to bite. Duck had sensitive skin and reacted strongly to people who handled her strongly. I learned to work with her softly, no hard curries or brushes on her skin.

Early in my relationship with her there was a woman who wanted to groom Ducky with me so she grabbed a brush. Ducky tensed immediately and I watched her move away from the woman. She was using a hard-bristled brush with a strong stroke and Ducky did not appreciate it. Ears back, tail swishing, Ducky swiftly moved away as far as she could, but the woman tried to follow. I intervened before Ducky took her objections to the next level.

She loved to make faces during grooming, stretching her face up to the sky and making camel-like faces with her lips. It was hysterical and I always knew when I found the right spot to itch on her neck. We'd stand in the barn aisle and she would rest her face on my shoulder. We'd just stay like that and breathe each other in, eyes closed, souls intertwined.

And I took my time – she was not a mare that appreciated being rushed! I recall a barn friend, Amanda, who could arrive after me, pull her gelding out, and be in the tack before I had Ducky's polos wrapped. It was impressive, but geldings are different. With a sensitive grey mare, one can only tack up so quickly! Anyway, I understood her. She had been handled roughly by some humans in her past, and so had I.

Ducky was a challenging and satisfying ride. A large mare, it could be hard to put her together and she naturally went very much on her forehand – balancing her and bring her back end under her was our goal. She was never mean or dishonest, but she was sometimes spooky and always complex.

My friend, Chris, and I switched horses once during a lesson. Chris's mare, Emma, was a much more petite 15-hand liver chestnut and when Chris hopped on Ducky, she compared her to a tank. Not sure Duck loved that, but it could seem like an accurate description at times! I was grateful every time I rode her, and she was healthy for most of her 29 years until the very end.

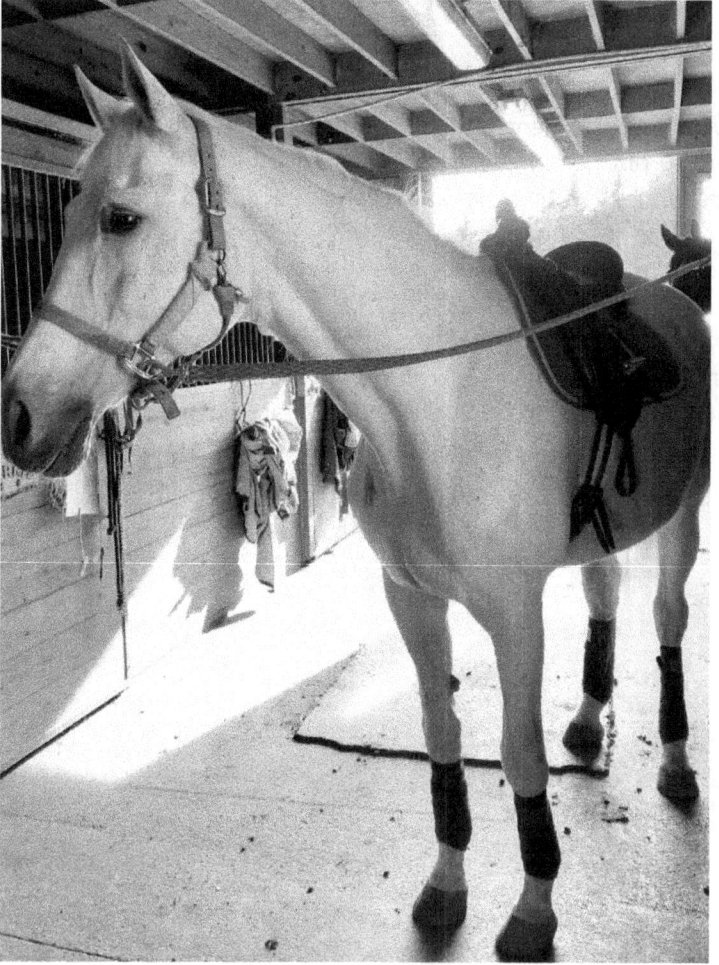

Ducky ready for a hack. Photo courtesy of author.

Ducky and Abi. Photo courtesy of author.

We spent six years together. Six years of Sunday afternoon rides, hand grazing in the sun, fiery walks from the upper barn, muzzle kisses, marathon grooming sessions, lessons, hacks with friends.

Convinced there were dragons, or maybe ghosts, in the far end of the indoor arena, we once spent an entire lesson walking past the rattling doors with my trainer holding her bridle and me in the irons. We overcame that and became better at managing her terror when ice and snow slid off the metal roof of the indoor. She still bolted (to be fair, the falling ice does sound like a freight train crashing overhead at times, startling human and horse alike).

But with Ducky I learned moving forward fixes everything, with horses and with life.

I had mounted for a lesson one evening in the early winter when it was first starting to get cold. This was early in my days of knowing Ducky. One of the students had tacked her up for me and used a quarter sheet due to the brisk night air.

A quarter sheet is a small blanket that covers the horse's loins, meant to be used while riding or warming up. It can be used tucked around a rider's legs or attached underneath the saddle. Most have a loop to go under the horse's tail to hold the sheet in place. This one had been attached under her saddle and tail, so it was not going anywhere.

As it turned out, Ducky had never worked in a quarter sheet before this and she Did. Not. Like. It. Not one bit. She took off around the arena and did her best imitation of a cow-cutting horse as she whipped around, snorting and tossing her mane in abject terror. I stayed with her, dropping into my seat and riding through it until I was able to stop her long enough to hop off. We did not use the quarter sheet again.

She was healthy until she wasn't, the last six weeks of her life were a blur of worry and vet visits. She was not able to get up when she laid down anymore, and horses need to be able to lie down to sleep.

It's true they can sleep standing up, but they need some amount of deep sleep, laying down sleep, most days. Horses are herd animals – one will often stay awake while the rest are asleep. That deep, REM sleep is necessary for them just like it is for us, and Ducky couldn't rest anymore.

We had to make the gut-wrenching decision to let her go and say goodbye.

That last day, I laid on the cold barn floor and held her face, my friend Kelley opposite me holding the other side of her, as she took her last breaths.

I inhaled her last exhale, and her soul come into mine. We were together, and we always would be. But when I lost her, I lost myself.

That cold day in December, holding her face, pressing my nose against hers, breathing her in like we always did, watching the warmth of her last exhalations, she saw me through her liquid brown eyes and knew the love surrounding her.

It was the sudden end no one asked for of a six-year relationship, longer and much more intense than I had experienced with most human partners. I struggled to breathe; shallow, insufficient breaths, and deep, ragged ones.

I was unmoored. I had lost my meaning. Restless, sleepless nights and cold, lonely days in a house and place where everything was sadness. It was all grey and darkness. I knew I could not stay. This would be my last New Year's Day in my old place.

A few months after I moved to Tampa, I stopped into my favorite secondhand furniture store. With a large showroom and high foot traffic, there is always something new to see. There wasn't anything I was looking for specifically that day, but we went in just to wander around.

In the very back room of the store, where they only have a few items and mostly use it to stage the rest of the store, I found a huge painting of a grey mare galloping, mane and tail flying, eyes bright. There was even a grey splotch on her right shoulder where Ducky had a dark spot.

It looks like I commissioned the painting; like it was made for me. I stood transfixed, staring, and crying, until my boyfriend picked up the painting and the pieces of my heart and helped me to the register. Her image hangs at the foot of my bed now, where I can see her and feel her spirit every day.

Chapter 4 – Leaving NY

Even after realizing I had to change my life to handle the awful new reality when Ducky died, I was still afraid to make the wrong choice. I had lived in New York my whole life. Leaving everything I knew was terrifying, even though I was excited for where I was going.

The familiarity of knowing the geography intimately and the comfort of having favorite hangouts is like a warm hug on a cold night.

Wrapped in safety, I had lived my life in this one place, complacent.

What if it wasn't worth risking all that?

For as long as I can remember, I have had this one image that would often come to mind when I was thinking of my future or when I was just sitting idly daydreaming.

My image is of a petite, sunny, plant-lined porch, all yellows and greens and natural woods, soft striped pillows and white pots suspended from the eaves filled with colorful flowers and trailing leafy vines.

Equally important as how it looks is the smell and feel of this place. It smells like summer, a soft hint of salt air with a light perfume of grass and flowers, and it feels like home.

In my vision, I'm there too, happy, relaxed, my blonde hair loosely tied up, casual clothes, skin warmed by the sun. I'm not sure when or why I started having this image, but it feels like it has been with me for a lifetime.

Yellow is the color of optimism, sunshine, and happiness. When I was going through the motions to relocate, this image kept popping into my mind and reassured me that moving to the tropics was the right idea; like it was meant to be.

Maybe I was chasing the carefree happiness.

Maybe it was the sun.

I listed my house for sale with the same agent I bought it from 15 years earlier. Ironically, his son had recently become a Realtor as well and helped with some of the sale details. He had been playing Little League the first go-round, and now was an adult helping guide my deal. Other than making me feel a little old, it was a nice experience to use the same Realtor; a bookend to my home ownership experience.

It was one way I found closure.

Letting go

Learning to let go is a constant challenge. As excited as I was to leave New York it was also heart-wrenching to leave my home. I had wanted different things when I got married so the letting go was not merely a physical loss of the house, but also a symbolic loss of the life I wanted to lead.

My American dream used to be the suburban house, dogs, picket fence, two-car lifestyle. But somewhere along the way that changed.

Or maybe it was me who had changed.

I had to let this image of my ideal life go, and mourn for that, even as that dream was replaced with new ones. This old image was built from a lifetime of assuming this was how my life would go, predictably, like my parents before me and theirs before them.

When I was younger, I didn't question it and fell into routine, thinking it was the only way to live. When I realized it wasn't working, I knew I had to let go.

Travel is one of my great passions in life and being lucky to have visited some diverse places has given me a new perspective on life and change and permanence.

I learned there is beauty everywhere if you look for it.

There are also lots of places I love, and for lots of different reasons. If I could fall in love with Amsterdam and London and New Orleans and San Diego, I knew I could find happiness living in a new place. I took comfort in that.

Travel has also taught me flexibility and to go with the flow. It has made me believe if I move and it's not perfect or I don't love it, I can adapt and find things I do like until I can move again. It doesn't have to be permanent; life is dynamic, and I take comfort in that.

Things will never be exactly like today again and I am willing to risk the possibility they will be even better.

In the last few months before I left New York, a series of encounters happened that made me think about closure and how to be okay about changing my life – and not only to be okay with changing, but to be exhilarated by the ever-changing nature of life.

I met a woman who owns a new coffeeshop in my city, a striking blonde named Katryn. She had recently started her business crafting fantastic lattes, juices, and pastries in a building her family owned, which she converted to a chic white and hot pink 80s-style space called Graham's filled with comfortable spots to sit and lots of bright windows.

I still dream about her pistachio lattes!

Katryn Malen. Photo courtesy of Katryn.

I spent a lot of time at Graham's drinking coffee, writing, and dreaming. I was setting up my business and Katryn's relaxing space and welcoming spirit let my creativity loose. I wrote most of my website sipping lattes at her coffee counter.

One morning as intoxicating hints of espresso and vanilla filled the cozy cafe, I was head down at my laptop sitting in my favorite spot at the bar. It was fall, and I was dressed in tall boots, skinny jeans, and a warm plaid scarf. A man and woman entered together, a puff of crisp autumn air following them inside. They were laughing and ordering coffees, and I laughed along at a joke the man made.

The woman glanced back at me sharply, exclaiming, "Abi?!?" I had a few moments of absolute panic trying to place her and finally apologized because I just could not remember who she was in the moment – ugh, one of the worst feelings in the world! She told me her name, that we knew each other in another life, in a galaxy far, far away.

Turns out, she was right. Heather and I had been classmates in our undergrad anthropology courses, and we hung around with the same group of friends, but close to two decades had passed since we last talked.

Back when we were co-eds, her boyfriend sold pot and Zeppelin was our usual soundtrack. Lots of people carried a hacky sack and Ultimate Frisbee on the quad was a thing. It was college in the 90s in upstate NY.

Heather and I had grown up from oversized flannels and Doc Martens and it was cool to catch up with her. After she left, I told Katryn how random and neat that was. She asked me what it meant. That was one thing I appreciated about Katryn; she understood things like this – that I was feeling *something* from seeing Heather.

I wasn't exactly sure what it was, but it seemed like more closure, like wrapping up old memories or perhaps reliving some nostalgia. I was thinking back about the old days and being grateful for their lessons, all while feeling ready and excited to move forward.

The next random thing was seeing my ex-boyfriend. And not just any ex, but, like *that* ex, everyone has one – the one that was almost the one, the one that felt different, the one that made you feel like you felt like you didn't exist on your own without him anymore. The one that said he was your soulmate, said he was head over heels for you, said no other woman made him feel like you did.

There is this beautiful old hotel in Albany called The Desmond. One of their restaurants, Simpson's, serves an incredible, traditional breakfast. The dining room is all dark woods, hunter greens, and cozy booths with hunting prints that fill the walls featuring gorgeous horses, country homes, and grassy hills. The food is amazing, and the service is even better.

It has always been one of my favorite places for breakfast. The omelets are fluffy, the hollandaise is fresh, and they serve a roasted tomato with your breakfast – a fancy nod to an English fry-up. I love it there and had to go one last time before leaving New York.

Over the years I lived in Upstate New York, I have introduced every boyfriend to the breakfast there. Most of them have also fallen in love with it.

On the morning I went for the last time I was filled with memories of so many breakfasts there with friends, family, and lovers. But I was thinking about that one ex-boyfriend in particular on the drive that morning. We had dated on and off for four years, and had shared many Desmond breakfasts. He was a man I would have stayed in New York for, at one point anyway.

Long after we had broken up, he still reached out over the years, dropping a birthday card or gift in my mailbox, or texting me and bringing Starbucks to my house, showing up uninvited, unwelcomed. I had been ignoring him for a while but once the For Sale sign was hanging in my front yard my anxiety kicked up. I worried he would contact me after seeing the listing or driving by and seeing the sign.

That day, setting off for the hotel in the cold November morning, I had an irrational idea he would be there having breakfast. The worry popped into my head, a little ripple of unease settling in among my thoughts of relocation and what to order in my omelet.

And then I walked into the restaurant and somehow, impossibly, he was there. Seated in a booth at the other end of the dining room, he was finishing his breakfast with someone else when I arrived. Having had this type of intuition my whole life, I wasn't exactly surprised to see him there.

Anyway, there he was and I laughed at the synchronicity.

This one felt expected; he had been a turning point in my life and the closure of seeing him one last time – and feeling nothing but relief – was powerful.

Sort of a "clearly you had to see him before leaving Albany" type thing. He was one of those guys I should not have dated, certainly not for four years, but I learned a lot about myself from it.

I am not sure if he saw me that last morning at the restaurant, or if he ever knew I was selling the house and leaving for good. I saw him, though, and it was final.

The last encounter was less random, but no less meaningful. In high school I dated Mike, and we stayed friends through my undergrad years. He is a drummer, and so funny, loyal, and kind. He had this red and grey pickup truck in high school, and we drove all over the countryside in that thing and had so much fun as kids.

Then life happened as it does. We drifted apart and existed solely as Facebook friends for years, commenting or liking each other's pics. Staying in that safe zone of sterile interactions and social media distance.

Mike was living about an hour from me, and I needed a plumber to fix a small leak when I was listing the house, so I asked him for a recommendation. Instead, he drove down and fixed it himself. Then we spent the next four hours laughing and reminiscing.

It was so cool to see him and talk about life then and now, remembering all those old high school memories I'd forgotten. To reconnect as adults with adult responsibilities and mortgages and fully formed opinions. The last time we spoke before that, we were still idealistic kids.

I had occasion to call Mike once more before I moved to ask for a favor and this kind man drove in freezing rain on a Sunday afternoon to help me load my bed and mattress into the Pod the night before it was being picked up. I had other help arranged but they had to cancel so I was scrambling because I had to get it loaded last into the container due to the Tetris packing game I was playing, and I was running out of time, as the Pod pickup was scheduled for the next morning.

Mike came over with no hesitation after spending his morning selling popcorn with his Boy Scout troop. Together we braved the cold rain to load the last of my things. I will be forever grateful for his friendship and help.

It was emotional and difficult to empty my house and load most of my physical things into the Pod, and it was also exciting and exhilarating.

Sharing some of those feelings with a close friend who knew me back when we were kids still learning about life together felt like the closure of this chapter.

Part Two

Changing

Chapter 5 – Learning to Manage Change

When I speak to audiences about change, I like to start by asking them how they feel about it, a quick gauge, a positive or negative gut check reaction. There is no right or wrong answer; rather it allows a chance to reflect for a moment about your feelings on change.

If you are reading this book, you likely already have some feelings about change.

So, take a moment now and answer that bellwether question for yourself: Do you feel positively or negatively about change? I'm forcing you to choose sides here, no ambivalent or neutral responses are allowed. Love it or hate it...

I have found audiences are often split 50/50, and while that answer is helpful to me as I speak to the group about change management, it is even more helpful to the individual participant to frame their initial position on change and start to think about moving that baseline.

Ask yourself why you feel the way you do. What has shaped your perceptions about change?

You might find you have not thought much about it.

Or maybe the basic discomfort of not knowing what is next is what you dislike.

Knowing your starting position on change, consider the different change management theories and models discussed in this chapter. Now aware of your own perceptions, you can begin to make small adjustments in how you approach change so that it becomes more comfortable for you.

We will examine three models in this chapter along with some practical ways you can apply them. Each of these models works well in a business setting too, so you can easily apply them to your team at work if you are implementing (or being faced with) a looming professional change.

In the next chapter, we will examine my own change model, the LEAP Change Model.

ADKAR

I liked using the ADKAR model at work when I was managing people and influencing stakeholders. I found I could also apply some of the concepts to help me as I worked through my own changes. ADKAR is a simple model. The acronym means Awareness, Desire, Knowledge, Ability, and Reinforcement.

First you need to be *aware* of the need for change, reinforcing early and often – even to yourself – why change is necessary. When change is forced on you, it can be more challenging since your awareness of the change may come at the same time as realizing you need to make the change. In those cases, focusing on the next steps is even more crucial.

Next up is desire – the *desire* to support the change is the 'what's in it for me' question. Define how the change benefits you and how life will be better after the change. This can be difficult when change has been imposed on you, so spending some time thinking of the positives will allow you to develop your desire to change.

Next is the *knowledge* of how to change. You may need to learn how to change and develop the skills (or *ability*) to implement the change. Lastly, reinforcement to make the change stick. When you get it right, celebrate! *Reinforcing* new behavior is key to making it last.

I use ADKAR to help clarify my thinking about a change. If I am working through the model, I usually am aware of and have the desire to change, so I spend more time in the middle of the model focused on skills, knowledge, and ability. This translates into research and asking questions for a change like relocation.

The model is simple to use as a writing and thought exercise and can be completed first to help you plan for and implement a change.

Kotter's 8-Step Process for Leading Change

Dr. Kotter developed his model after studying the way organizations and individuals managed change. He put together his eight-step process for leading change. I like the way this model focuses on garnering excitement for change. It is a little different from the other models discussed here, but there are similarities, too.

Kotter's first step is to create urgency by helping others see the need for change. He recommends going as far as writing a mission or vision statement for the change – an aspirational opportunity statement.

This statement acts as a motivator and sustainer for when you are slogging through the depths of the change and feeling overwhelmed; a "quit-detractor," if you will. This works for both changes you want to make and those imposed on you. The going can get tough with both kinds of change and adding an extra layer of motivation can be the push you need.

Step two is building a guiding coalition. This is where you recruit help to guide your change. Perhaps it is asking experts, whether mentors or Google experts; or talking to a trusted friend or partner. In business, this is getting a few key stakeholders to commit to making change to advance the goals.

Step three is forming a strategic vision and initiatives. This is where you clarify how the future will look different from the current state after the change. Spell out in detail how to make the future a reality. This is a game plan of sorts, and you can make it as detailed as you need.

Step four is enlisting a volunteer army of supporters. I already talked about some of the people who stepped in to help me when I was relocating, and I will introduce other characters throughout this book.

Some of my supporters helped me research Tampa, while others helped finish chores and updates at my house in New York. One helped me move my things from a storage unit to my home, another helped load a heavy dresser in the Pod. Who is in your volunteer army?

Step five is enabling action by removing barriers. What are the things holding you back from moving forward and making the change you want in your life? Are these barriers actual limitations or are they created in your mind?

Sometimes we get too deep in our heads and assume challenges exist or are greater than they are. It can be difficult to see the end when all we see are the hardships along the way. If there are actual barriers, however, it's best to remove those you can. In this step, identify potential barriers to change and decide how to circumvent them if they pop up.

Step six is all about the wins! This is where you generate (and celebrate) short-term wins, especially those early ones. Recognizing and celebrating small successes along the way is vitally important to staying motivated. Humans are motivated by positive reinforcement. Celebrating a win brings renewed energy and enthusiasm to keep going.

Step seven is sustaining acceleration. After a win, Kotter advises to push harder. It can be tempting to sit back and rest on our laurels after a win, but that is the time to leap in harder and keep going. Start a kaizen, or habit, of change after change after change. That is one way to build sustainability into your change habit.

Kotter's last step, step eight, is about ensuring the change is adopted. This is where you practice until you get it right and make it last. There were days in the relocation process that were tough; days I did not want to continue. I almost quit after getting laid off, finding it easier to stay in bed than to pack, paint, clean, and market my house and myself.

'Progress not perfection' is what made me get out of bed. I thought if I could do a little bit, one tiny piece or step, check one thing off the perennial To-Do list, I would be better off.

Progress, not perfection; make a little forward progress and eventually it happened where those small steps added up. Bigger goals would be accomplished and I would celebrate them, which made me want to work harder so I could celebrate more. Pretty basic, and it worked for me.

McKinsey's 7-S Model

McKinsey's model shows the seven internal elements that must be aligned for success to happen. The seven elements, or S's, include strategy, structure, systems, shared values, skills, style, and staff. McKinsey created the model for use in organizations, but I find it is relevant in personal applications too, because it helps to visualize how altering one aspect or lever affects the other areas.

The model shows each of the seven elements (S's) connected to each other and is a great representation of the interconnectedness of different aspects of life. When one element is changed, the others change in response.

It is the interconnectivity of the pieces of the model that intrigued me about McKinsey's work. Each element must work in concert with all the others. Making a slight tweak pulls the strings of the other facets of life. This is extremely simple and yet so profound to me. If my work life is unsatisfying, it affects all the other aspects.

If I am lonely and missing a partner – that basic human connection and intimacy – it brings the other parts of my life out of focus. Each part in harmony – that is a powerful lesson from this model. Making major life changes will affect every part, and maintaining a balance is important.

Learning to Trust the Change Continuum

The good news for me is that I learned that change and the different choices you could make are generally not opposites of each other. Meaning, one outcome is not likely to be the worst possible outcome with the other choice being the best possible result.

Outcomes exist on a continuum, where it is much more likely that choice A will be slightly better than choice B; or even more realistically, both choice A and B will have positive aspects and each can overshadow some qualities of the other in some ways.

The following illustration depicts the change continuum. Both choices will fall somewhere on the continuum, with one leaning more on the positive side. Plotting your options on the continuum may help you decide, or simply feel reassured that both choices you may make are appealing ones with positive attributes.

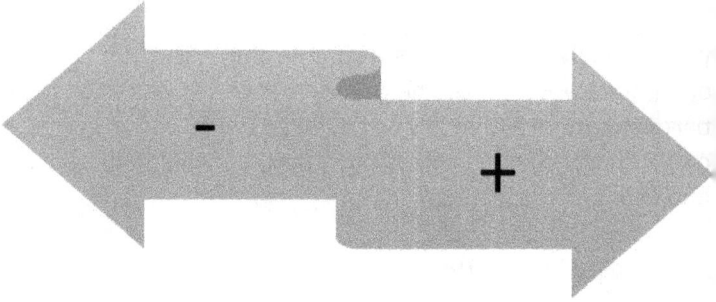

Once I learned to trust the change continuum, it changed the way I made decisions.

I had the confidence to say yes to new things knowing I'd be happy with my choice.

When I was deciding where to move, I knew a few key things. I was craving a warmer, sunnier climate, and since I could pick anywhere in the US, I wanted to pick a state with better tax benefits. With a few other considerations in play, I narrowed it to Tampa, Florida or Austin, Texas.

I settled in South Tampa, but had I picked Austin I know I would also be falling in love with Texas right about now! I would be wearing my Ariat's and going to see live country music more often, maybe trading my dressage saddle for a Western one.

But as it happens, I'm going to the beach and watching tropical sunsets over the bay, looking for dolphins and manatees and alligators, and finding gorgeous places to hang a hammock. I think I'm happier in Tampa, but I know I would have found happiness if I'd decided on Austin, too.

The change continuum works even when it's a change pushed on you, like getting laid off. Taking back some control by identifying your options and placing them on the change continuum can show you things are not all terrible and there is good to be found within each option.

It was liberating for me to look at my options in terms of which was slightly better than the other, instead of worrying one was going to ruin me while the other choice would be fantastic. That "all-or-nothing" thinking style is paralyzing.

Sometimes we get caught up thinking that things will go back to the way they used to be, the way they always were, if we wait long enough. This is an application of the normalcy bias and it can be damaging in relation to change.

When a change happens, it's easy to convince yourself that things will ultimately go back to normal, instead of being open to the idea that the change is now the *new* normal. Understanding and accepting this idea lets you move forward from the new starting point, with all the corresponding opportunities and challenges.

It's not going back the way it was. Better to accept that and accept the way things are now – instead of wasting time waiting for things to return to the old normal.

New Opportunities

The best way I found to manage change within myself was to shift my thinking. Realizing that regardless of the change, even a change I found negative on the surface, there were new opportunities that did not exist before. I only had to look for them.

57

Leaning into the newness let me see options and possibilities everywhere, and often, when you look for something, you find it. It reminds me of one of my favorite Winston Churchill quotes: "A pessimist sees difficulty in every opportunity, an optimist sees opportunity in every difficulty." Approaching change with this mentality has let me find joy in challenge and excitement in the newness.

A quick reminder about change management and using these models to help you through the process: Do not be discouraged when you find yourself working through the various feelings that arise in you. You will have highs and lows, and sometimes the lows feel awful. Called the 'valley of despair' for a reason, these lows can be challenging.

But know it always gets better.

Chapter 6 – The LEAP Change Model

Working through so many monumental changes in a short time made me start thinking differently. I realized that there was something lacking in each change management model I studied.

So, I created my own change management model focusing on the areas I think are most important. This model has helped me greatly through some heavy life changes.

I named my model the LEAP Change Model in celebration of my habit of leaping in. In life and in change models alike, simple is elegant and efficient. I like its ease of use. This model is easy to remember, making it particularly helpful when you're under pressure.

LEAP

The LEAP Change Model is simple – and through its simplicity the model provides clarity.

LEAP stands for Learn, Engage, Act, and Practice. One thing to remember before we dig in: the LEAP Change Model is intended to be fluid. You are free to move between the steps at your own pace, moving back a phase or forward at your discretion. You are in control of your pace and how you utilize this model.

Learn

The first step of my change model is to learn – learn everything you can about the change, yourself, how you feel about it, how others feel about it. Clearly identify the change. If you cannot, this is a good place to spend some time. What are the key aspects of the change? How do you need to go about accomplishing it?

This could be considered your research step and you should be as exhaustive as you need to be. Some changes require considerably more research than others and how long you spend at the learning stage is up to you. This does take a little subjectivity. You've learned enough when you feel like you've learned enough. Trust yourself, you will know when it is enough.

I like to use my journal to write and plot and brainstorm on paper. You could use your laptop if it suits you better. I also like to buy a large piece of posterboard, like the kind you bought as a kid for school presentations, the kind that is white with one shiny side and one matte side.

I have a set of gorgeous colored markers and I sit with the posterboard and set a timer for 15 minutes. And then I have at it – I use one color for the main idea and different vibrant colors for smaller sub-ideas spiraling off from the main thought.

I love to brainstorm this way. The end result is a colorful, messy, beautiful visualization of dotted lines connecting thoughts and randomness everywhere and new ideas popping up. I don't edit myself during this process – anything and everything goes on the paper. It probably looks crazy but that's how my brain works during a brainstorm session!

If the timer runs out and I am still going, I simply extend it another 15 minutes. The idea behind the timer is simply to keep myself somewhat grounded as I could get lost in thought for an afternoon without noticing until the shadows on the wall mark sundown. This helps me to learn and think and project everything I can about the change.

One caveat, though – sometimes it is easy to convince yourself you need more and more information. After all, knowing more is better, right? But sometimes that relentless search for data points to graph leads to inaction. You could spend forever at the learning stage, which is the opposite of your change goal.

Creating a sense of urgency in yourself is important. Remember why you want to make a change and let yourself be excited about it! This is the time to think big, immerse yourself in your why, and leap in!

Engage

The next step is engage – engage yourself and engage others who will help you. Make a list of people who can help you. Alternatively, make a list of the help you need. Sometimes throwing money at the situation is the right answer – if you do not have the right help in your circle and you have a specialized need, hire an expert.

One example of this was hiring my Realtor to sell my house. Not only did he manage the sale, but he also handled the marketing, photos, ideas to fix it up, administrative tasks, and legal issues.

Most importantly, engage yourself. How do you get pumped up and excited for change? Maybe it is listening to upbeat music or watching an inspirational TED Talk. Whatever your go-to is, do it now and do it often during change! Make sure you remain engaged and excited! If you are not passionate about your change, no one else will be.

Spend time to clearly define how life will be better after your change. What are the things you are most looking forward after the change dust settles? What will be better, what stays the same, what has to change next? Know what's in it for you. This is critical to your engagement in the long run.

You may wish to draft a motivational statement here, something of a vision or mission statement. Putting your intention into words is powerful. Restating it as you get tired can be the push you need to get through the tougher times when change loses its shiny newness.

Another way to engage is to ask questions. There is a root-cause problem-solving tool called the '5 Whys' which has practitioners ask why in a series of progressively deeper probes to peel back layers and drill down to the root cause.

Asking yourself questions keeps you curious and learning. It may feel like you are shifting between the learn and engage phase here and that is ok; you are still moving forward.

Working through a change management process can be difficult. One way to re-energize your brain is to try doing things in a different way.

If you do not typically make lists or write down steps to your goals, try it. You may find working in a new way is more efficient for you or perhaps it forces you to be present in the change work again. Either way it is a win.

Act

The third step is act – planning is important but at some point, you need to leap in and act. Now is the time. Remember back to To-Do lists and checklists. How can you frame the change into actionable steps? Concrete action items are your goal in this step.

This is the step where you are getting the bulk of your work finished. For me, with my relocation, it involved, for example, loading the Pod, moving boxes to U-Haul, and driving across the country with Sasha. These were all (huge) action steps. Smaller, but still exciting, steps included getting rid of non-essential items from the house and painting the back porch.

Sometimes it is better to do something than nothing. You may not think you are making much progress but it all adds up. When a change has been purely theoretical for a long time, like my relocation was, any action heartily beats inaction.

It is a cliché that the first step is the hardest. You make it more difficult in your mind than it is. We build things up so much that taking a first step is terrifying. It is always bigger and scarier in your head, though. And once you take one step, it is easier to take the next one and so on. Movement creates momentum.

If you find you are having a hard time taking that first step into action, consider why. What is holding you back? This may take reflection or meditation, but the why is important. If it is a barrier for you, it is better to determine why and resolve it. After, you can move forward.

Practice

Reinforcing new habits requires practice to make the change constant in your life. This is when you need to practice and program yourself with your new habit. It can take time to become comfortable with change and let the newness burn off. Give yourself the grace to make mistakes and the time to build new habits.

Change is hard work and results are not often found immediately. But over time, practice builds habits; and by focusing on progress over perfection you will see positive results sooner than you think. Be patient with yourself and take as long as you need.

Part of my practice includes rewarding myself when it is going well. Building in breaks and celebrations is important to keeping the momentum alive. Breaking tasks, notably difficult and long ones, down into smaller parts and celebrating the completion of those parts helps me stay driven and focused.

During the practice step, spend some time to debrief. Think about what went well and what you would have done differently – a post-mortem or after-action review. Reflecting and considering how to be better next time helps you develop a habit of continuous improvement – priming you to make changes easier and less stressful in the future. If change is not a stressor for you, perhaps you too will decide to leap in!

Finally, think about sustainability in this last step. Plan how you will maintain your new state of being. What are the ways you can ensure lasting change?

How to use the LEAP Change Model

The LEAP Change Model works well for both personal and organizational changes. I like to use it when I'm first deciding to make a change and establishing the framework going forward.

My goal is to first spend time thinking about the change and then to begin using the model, but sometimes you do not have the gift of time. In that case, focus more on the Learn stage to be certain you are ready to begin changing.

Learn and *engage* can be simultaneous phases, or you may see some overlap or back and forth. Right when you think you are moving forward you may recall some research you forgot to do. Just like that, you are back to the learn stage, but not for long. It is a fluid, dynamic process.

How long you spend at each step is up to you. The important part is making the model suit you and your individual change needs. It was created to be adaptable.

Hanging out in the practice phase for a while can be a good habit as well. It is useful to continue reinforcing new skills, so practicing after you have implemented a change can help it stick. Long-term change can take time, so lingering in the practice step where you reinforce, celebrate, and recognize your success is a great place to be.

One good way to use the LEAP Change Model is to share it with others. You may have started to do this during the engage phase, so you can continue that work and share what you are working on with your support team. Talking about goals and plans can help shift them into reality and it is the same with your change management strategy. Other people see gaps we do not and help us develop our fragmented thoughts and partial ideas into well-formulated theories.

Some call this gathering your tribe, finding your group, or picking your people. This is your circle of close confidants: friends, partners, siblings, lovers, colleagues; those people close to you that you trust inherently. You may have one or two or three people in this group – small is fine.

My closest friends, Ramya, Elaine, and Denise, are people I consider in this group. We text each other to ask opinions, share good news and scary things, and support each other's business ventures. They are the people I'd call day or night to celebrate with or cry with. They think my boyfriend looks like a racecar driver and I think their lives are simply incredible.

Denise is an incredible mentor and role model – a hiker, business mogul, mother, traveler, and free thinker. She has taught me poise, balance, and depth. Watching her in action has inspired me to be more thoughtful in business and life.

Elaine is the most energetic networker, the one who always asks the challenging questions without fear, and undoubtedly one of the most ambitious, hardest-working women I know. She has brought me further than I ever thought I would go and has encouraged me to become a better leader. She and her husband, John, are kind, thoughtful, generous souls.

And Ramya – my gorgeous Ramya, who is brilliant, beautiful, and bold. She makes it look easy to balance a challenging career, energetic twins, and moves across the world while being an amazing friend, wife, and human being. She makes me laugh when I want to cry and supports everything I do with her whole being.

Finding these women was immensely important to me. I had never had this type of support system, so it was different for me to embrace it at first. I had to change how I approached people and relationships. I had to learn these were people who genuinely wanted to support me and each other and the great ideas that were flowing in the group.

We amplify each other, bring out the best in each other, and challenge each other to do more and think deeper.

Having this group of supporters in your life will be immeasurably helpful as you navigate change. They can be your sounding board as you learn and can even help you with research and asking the right questions.

Engaging them by talking about your change will engage you even more, and when you go to take action they can go along for the ride. Celebrating and practicing your new habit with them is a no-brainer.

Friends are the best to celebrate your wins.

Elaine, Abi, Ramya in Manhattan. Photo courtesy of author.

Elaine and Abi, circa 2018. Photo courtesy of author.

Chapter 7 – Resilience

Resilience is defined in two distinct ways by the Oxford Dictionary:

1. the capacity to recover quickly from difficulties; toughness

2. the ability of a substance or object to spring back into shape; elasticity

The first definition is probably the one you think of in relation to resilience in a person or company, thinking about one's ability to bounce back when bad things happen, or how emotionally tough a person appears to be. But the second definition deserves some consideration, as well. Essentially, it is saying resilience is how rapidly you can get back to normal after a bad event, or back into your usual form.

Elasticity can be a physical trait, or it can describe your ability to change when things change. Going with the flow...except that term makes it feel passive when it is anything but. You are bending when circumstances change and require it, bouncing back to your usual form when circumstances allow it. Considering yourself elastic lets you bend when needed and come back to yourself, perhaps even springing back into a better version of you.

Ups and Downs

The year of my move and layoff afforded plenty of opportunities to practice resilience and perfect the art of being elastic. The year started slow and steady with lots of little steps forward and back; cleaning, painting, clearing out storage areas, getting rid of things.

The graph was trending up steadily, nothing to worry about. It started moving more erratically when I engaged the Realtor and made some big (read, expensive!) improvements to the house, like painting most of the interior. Some financial hits and ups and downs happened while working with contractors, and the graph fluctuated more wildly.

My house went on the market – a definite high – and showings began. Each showing was exciting but it was followed by a let-down when a prospective buyer didn't make an offer. Next the layoff happened; a huge downswing in my 2019 graph. And then the next day when I received the first offer on my house, oh wow, it was a dizzying uptick!

After that, again lots of little ups and downs. The house needed a few things post-inspection and I had to negotiate and settle on some items. I signed the lease on my first apartment in 15 years – an incredible place in Tampa and that was a remarkably high point on my graph. I scored a gorgeous bay view, two-bedroom in Westshore that I totally fell in love with!

I've watched as the sky turns to a gorgeous kaleidoscope of sunset colors from my balcony in the last year more often than I ever have in my life. I hashtag most posts #luckygirl and #baylife and #changeyourlife.

I left New York a few days before my planned closing. Over the next few weeks as I settled into Tampa life, there was delay after delay with the house closing coming from the buyer. I couldn't get a straight answer from the attorneys and my realtor was also struggling to find out what was happening.

Finally, one evening he texted me that the buyer's agent told him they had the clear to close and we would move forward and schedule the closing the next day. Incredible high! The next morning, I dropped back down amazingly low as my attorney told me the deal had fallen through. In the end, the buyer couldn't secure their funding.

I was crushed, absolutely floored that this was even possible – naïve, perhaps, but I had believed the experts working with me that the deal was secure going into closing. It was awful, almost as bad a low as getting laid off. I cried – ugly dramatic tears and slow quiet ones that burned in the night.

But I was elastic, I knew I would spring back somehow. And I did. My realtor took new, wintry pics of the house and updated the listing to promote it again. We had a flurry of showings and a second offer, this time a more secure one, according to my attorney's office.

Leaping in again, I accepted the second offer and we moved to close. The second time around, closing was a much calmer process. One warm Florida night in February I got news from snowy New York that the deal was finalized, the closing was complete, and the house had been transferred to its new owner.

I hoped they were sitting by my old fireplace, toasting their success, and dreaming of a new life in their new home as I was sitting on my new balcony listening to the bay, dreaming of the same.

I hoped they would love it as much as I did and pour all their dreams into its walls.

I hoped they were happy there.

I hoped.

Ways to be resilient

I found lots of ways to stay resilient through all these ups and downs, some more successful than others. I have always been a fan of checklists and To-Do lists; they keep me sane and it is very satisfying to cross something off a To-Do list.

Pro tip: break tasks down into smaller steps and add them to your To-Do list, and you can feel accomplished, celebrate a little win, and be motivated to keep going when you get to cross a step off your list.

Checklists helped me organize things I needed to do, like getting a Pod to move my things or all the steps to leasing a new place. I am a planner by nature so making lists, plans, and breaking steps into smaller To-Do lists came instinctively to me and calmed me at the same time. These tools forced me to be resilient because I had to keep going to stay on track and keep crossing things off.

I like Gantt charts and calendar systems in general, both of which can be used with checklists and To-Dos to help keep on track and stay elastic. You can only suffer a setback for so long if you are going to stay on target and knowing that helped me focus when things did go wrong.

Progress over perfection is one of my favorite sayings. It has helped me get so many things accomplished by just taking one step, doing something even if it is not perfect or complete or finished. If I did not start somewhere and take some small bit of action, I would never accomplish anything.

Another thing that helped me to stay resilient was leaning on friends who had gone through a cross-country relocation themselves. Talking to those who had been there was hugely important for me.

My friend, Mike, is another Floridian who transplanted from Chicago. He gave me hope and positivity when I needed it, reminding me of the reasons why life would be better after the move, or at least that I could wear shorts year-round.

Another friend, Marty, had relocated from Pennsylvania to Austin a few months before my move and was a source of inspiration for me in my move as he is in life. Both Mike and Marty made big moves and were happy after their moves. If they could do it, so could I.

Ramya and Elaine both relocated to the United States after growing up in other countries and have since made several moves around the US. Their bravery has always humbled me. Knowing they did it helped me stay focused on the end goal even when the ups were slow to come and the downs were constant.

I made sure to celebrate small wins along the way, as recommended in the various change models discussed earlier. Humans are motivated by positive reinforcement, so celebrating a small accomplishment and checking it off the To-Do list motivated me to keep going and get more and more small wins. Eventually those add up and you have accomplished the major things.

A few small wins I celebrated along the way included when I finished packing the Pod; when I finished the move out of the U-Haul storage unit; when I signed the lease on my new apartment in Tampa; the end of garage sale weekend in New York; and passing into each new state on the drive from New York to Florida.

When writing this book, I celebrated when I passed 10,000 words, which coincidentally happened in this paragraph. Take a moment, let's celebrate something together! What are you proud of in this moment? And go! Little mini celebration, just us, right here and right now.

There! That felt good :)

Mindfulness

When you are caught up in a whirl of emotions during a monumental change in your life, it can be hard to focus your mind. One trick I learned is practicing mindfulness. For me, this means being in the moment and truly feeling and experiencing an emotion or situation. I have always liked to walk and getting in a couple of miles daily has always been a respite for me, a way to relieve stress.

But when I was encumbered by thoughts of relocation, the details of the house sale, the minutia of packing and cleaning, I found I could take my afternoon walks and not remember a thing about them. Not the feel of the air or the neighbors I passed, no sounds of birds or traffic or distant train horns.

I was not feeling refreshed from my walks and wasn't feeling the thrill of being outside and moving. I wasn't *feeling*. It's the same thing you do when you drive a familiar route, except I wanted to zone *in* on my walks, not zone *out*.

I decided to try being mindful on my walks. At every block or street crossing, I reminded myself to pause, look around, and feel. I tried engaging all my senses to find something I smelled, touched, heard, and saw (not so much tasted!), and to notice that thing - whether it was the way the leaves crunched underfoot or the sun shining on the snow.

It was a practice; sometimes I was more successful than others, and when I was, I loved being able to leave my thoughts and experience the world. It made me enjoy my walks more and made me notice my gratitude and happiness.

When I was a teen, I worked at the barn with my friends. One day in the height of summer, when everything is bright green and the air hangs still and thick, dusty from passing hooves, Gina and I were bringing in a pair of horses from turnout. Pausing to let them grab a few last mouthfuls of grass, we wiped the sweat and dirt from our faces, the afternoon sun relentless in its glow.

She was holding Beau, our trainer's leggy charcoal English thoroughbred, a regal gentleman who embodied his elegant name Beau Royale. I had his best friend in my hands, Damascus, a gorgeous tall, bay warmblood with incredible presence and movement.

Damascus was always one of my favorite horses to watch in work. He was classically trained in Europe, like my gelding, and had impeccable timing. His passage and half-pass were near perfect, floating movements across the school.

That hot July afternoon in the blazing sun with the sweaty geldings, sighing in frustration at the heat, Gina asked me if I could remember right then what winter felt like, what it actually felt like to be cold.

Could I imagine it, that feeling of being freezing cold, chilled to your bones, even as we were stood, swatting away horseflies and watching the sweat run off each other's faces? And I thought about it for a minute, in the midday July sun, absently scratching the grazing horse's withers, and I realized that I could feel it.

For a moment, when I really tried, really focused, I could feel the shock of the cold air stinging my cheeks and taking my breath away, and the feeling of a chill rising into my boots from the frigid concrete barn floor, and of snowflakes on my eyelashes and melting on my nose. I could make myself *feel* it.

Closing my eyes, I was transported to a wintry land, the snow drifting in the wind and the sun glaring off white snowscapes, with icicles hanging from trees and soft thumps in the woods as snow slid from pine boughs and hit the ground. I could almost hear the car tires crunching the snow and see the horses' breath in the cold morning air. Damascus' coat was short and thin now, but I could imagine a time near Christmas when the long, soft hairs would be so thick I could bury my fingers in it and warm my hands.

Yoga has often helped me find my focus and purpose as well, and I tried to at least practice a sun salutation occasionally during this year of change. A few years ago, I was traveling every week for work doing lean management consulting.

A fun time, for sure, but the travel caught up to me. I spent time in St. Louis and Charlotte, commuting back to New York on the weekends. I had a boyfriend at home then. He and I were having problems, and it was never meant to be a forever thing, but the ending was still sad.

I regularly went to Wednesday night class in Charlotte at an amazing studio where I first tried aerial yoga among other things (Be Yoga, thank you!). It was there that I figured out something was very wrong. I would lay in sav asana after practice and cry quietly in the dark studio. Every. Single. Time.

I had never broken down in tears during yoga before, and it became a perplexing pattern. I ultimately figured out it was a place I was so relaxed and comfortable that I could be myself and feel my emotions. It made me realize I was terribly unhappy and had to make changes, the first of which was ending my relationship.

Crying at yoga was only the start, though. (Seriously, who cries in yoga? But if you do, too, think about why...this could be life-changing.) Realizing in those moments in the dark when I let my mind freely wander and my body relax, when I let go of what I am supposed to do and be and think, when I am just me without worrying about what others think of that, realizing then in those depths of reflection that I was deeply unhappy brought me to change.

Well, first it brought me to tears, then to a need to make changes in my life and to live my life in a way that was truer to me. I had spent my life trying to be who I thought I should to please parents, teachers, boyfriends, colleagues, everyone but myself, and failing miserably at being happy while doing it.

This was not how I was going to live going forward, though.

A last thought about resilience. Sometimes it really is simply about putting your head down and pushing through.

Grit. Mental toughness. Determination.

Whatever you want to call it, you have heard it before and can probably remember a time in your life when you had to keep going even though you wanted to quit, and it was hard and not fun.

Accounting classes in grad school were one of those moments for me. The good news is if you can remember that time it means you did it and you can do it again.

Knowing you have been successful before can be the motivator to help you push through again, keeping in mind that the first definition of resilience is toughness.

Chapter 8 – Making Moves

Relocating took about a year. The different parts of the process taking different amounts of time, but overall, my preparations through unpacking was one year of hard work.

The Prep

All the other stages passed in a heartbeat, where the prep stage seemed to last forever. Maybe it was because I thought about moving and making big changes for a long time before I did it. Maybe it really was a long phase, but either way I learned the most during this stage.

My house was a small ranch built in the 1950s. I had updated many things in my 15 years there, and other things were a little outdated. I was never one to collect a lot of things or keep knick-knacks or collections of things around, but I still had accumulated a ton of stuff over the years.

Closet by closet, drawer by drawer, I emptied the house of unnecessary things, cleaning as I went. My insomnia was bad during this year of change so I would be up in the middle of the night, cleaning a room or straightening a closet or painting a shelf. It was not healthy, but it worked, at least for a little while.

I sold lots of things on Facebook marketplace, meeting people in public if the item was transportable, and moving it outside to meet people in the yard if it was too large for my Mini Cooper. My heavy winter parka was exciting to sell and getting rid of things like my backyard grill and a large dining room table were necessary for the move.

I was so excited to sell my cute red desk to a friend from grad school to give to her stepdaughter. It was an adorable and very sturdy LL Bean desk I had loved for years, and I was thrilled to both see my friend again and to know a little girl would enjoy my desk and grow up using it.

I also held a garage sale one blustery early November weekend, summoning to my yard the fifth circle of hell. I did not plan to have a garage sale but ended up with more little things than expected after cleaning out the shed and attic. I do not ever plan to do it again: 0/5, do not recommend!

But I sold lots of things and donated the rest. The most exciting was when my neighbor, Todd, came over to chat and say goodbye and I gave him my rakes and snow shovels. I may have danced my way back inside when he left!

I relied on checklists, To-Do lists, and grit during the Prep. It was the winter of my relocation. I was still working full-time and riding horses, so my time was limited and my energy low. It was about keeping going, reaching one small goal, moving to the next, and not stopping.

82

The U-Haul

It was clear to me early on that I did not have enough space in my house to adequately stage it for sale with the requisite almost-empty closets and sparsely arranged furniture, so I rented a storage unit at U-Haul.

Luckily, it was right down the street from my house and I made many trips with my Mini Cooper filled to the brim. Quite literally over the brim, I suppose, as I would put the top down on the convertible, fill it with boxes and bags and random sundries, and drive to U-Haul and unload.

It was there that I met B., someone who ended up helping me tremendously, albeit unexpectedly. He worked at U-Haul and sold me my unit. I saw him there often in my many trips to move boxes into the unit and always waved to him. When I knew I was moving out of the unit, I told him my plans to empty it and he told me he would have a truck that night and he would help me move out.

I came to U-Haul after work that snowy November night, and B. had a moving truck and moved all my things from the storage unit to the truck, then followed me to my house and unloaded all the boxes into the house. He did it to be nice and to help me, a virtual stranger he met a few months ago.

I was amazed when he left that night with only a thank you, making no other demands of me. B. was a friend to me when I needed someone to help me. I was used to doing everything by myself, and I learned to accept help along the relocation, starting with B.

The Sale

My house was on the market almost 30 days when I accepted the first offer. During that time, there were lots of showings and an open house. I left for the showings, of course, packing my cat in the Mini and taking her for a drive if she was restless or to sit at the church down the street if she was calm.

Sasha has always been a good traveler and is more adaptable than many cats. I traveled lots during her kittenhood, so she became best friends with the staff at the vet's office where she stayed overnights

Sasha in a basket.

She refused to leave the house only once when a showing was scheduled, hiding inside a chaise lounge chair where she ignored my desperate pleas for her to come out. After that, she came willingly each time.

I fell into a routine of cleaning nightly and picking up after myself and Sasha during the days. It was stressful, and my insomnia took over. Waking up at 2 or 3 a.m. and worrying became my normal.

The Pod

I decided to use a Pod to move the bulk of my stuff. I was storing some things at my parents' house in North Carolina and would move some important and fragile things in the Mini when I made the drive, but the furniture I was taking and most of my personal items were going in the Pod.

I had one week with the Pod sitting in my driveway to load it. It turned out to be exactly the right size for me, and gradually I filled it with boxes, clothes, shoes, furniture, and the rest of my things.

My friend, Larry, helped me move my huge antique dresser into the Pod one night and Mike came to help load my bed and box spring the night before the Pod pickup.

The Pod itself became a metaphor for the relocation; just like the move, I didn't know if the Pod was the right choice or if it would be the right fit or if I would end up with lots of broken dreams and dishes in Tampa, but I was leaping in and trying.

I have never been one for long road trips. My need to pee often coupled with my intense hatred of traffic and other drivers and general inability to focus for long periods of time made long drives my nemesis.

The longest I had driven previously in one trip was 16 hours round trip to Pittsburgh and back in an overnight, but that wasn't for me, that was for a dear friend's mother's funeral, a trip made mostly on autopilot and fueled by grief.

Driving across the country was something I never imagined I could do.

But then I did.

There is no real magic there - it was about getting it done, one mile then the next. Because I had Sasha in her crate whenever we were in the car, I did not want to go much more than six or seven hours each day. My parents' house in North Carolina was a good halfway point, although I was too exhausted and focused on my end goal to make the visit long.

Leaving New York in December meant the possibility of bad weather for the first two days of the trip, something that I was dreading in my Mini Cooper convertible. There was snow and freezing rain on and off for the first day, and I think Pennsylvania was the toughest driving on the trip.

As I traveled south, winter held a stubborn icy grip over the landscape until I was close to Delaware and Maryland. Shedding layers of clothing and turning down the heat in the car I drove south, drinking coffee and singing loudly to Morphine and Britney Spears I got closer and closer.

Sasha settled in quickly in Tampa.

Sasha is a chatty cat and a total momma's girl and she meowed and purred as we drove, my fingers in her crate resting on her back or tail when I was not shifting. This trip was big for me, so I tried for mindfulness, to remember the drive and to experience it, but I was too excited most of the time.

South Carolina was pretty, entering Georgia was exciting, and passing into Florida was a thrill. I woke Sasha whooping in exhilaration when I saw my first Florida palm tree!

In four days of driving, one year of preparation, and a lifetime of dreaming, I had gone from parka to playa, blizzard to beach, snow to surf.

Goodbye, Abi with MetLife from New York.

Meet the new Abi from Tampa. She's happy and a writer and loves the beach and... who knows how that sentence will go on?

Shrugging off the shadows of my past and speeding into my future; top down, sun shining, girl beaming.

The Unpack

I'll be honest here, the unpack was a blur. Four days of driving with the fuzzball in the car – which makes me a nervous driver worrying that even the slightest accident would be a big deal for her – and I was exhausted.

When I parked outside the apartment building and saw Mark I finally relaxed. He took care of everything, single-handedly unloading the Pod. I live in a third-floor walk-up and somehow he – by himself –

carried up a full mattress and box spring, bed frame, bookshelves boxes filled with my hardcover Dean Koontz collection, all my shoes...

Mark prioritized getting my bed set up so Sash and I could nap. I protested as he marched me into the bedroom. No way could I fall asleep. The view, the sun, being with him, the newness of this life! He insisted we try anyhow, and somehow sleep took over and my mind shut down.

For two glorious hours we slept while Mark unloaded the entire Pod and did his best to put things where they might belong.

I woke up in time for my first Tampa Bay sunset with him, and they – and he! – have not stopped thrilling me since that first night.

Part Three

Becoming

Chapter 9 – Everything New

Even the sky seems bigger in Tampa. The part of New York I am from is a strikingly beautiful place, mountains and escarpments and valleys carved from the slow passage of ancient glaciers and the persistent flow of rivers over time.

With the Catskills to the south, the Adirondacks up north, and the Helderbergs all around, the part of New York State I called home for the last two decades was enclosed by gorgeous mountains and lakes and forests and streams.

Thanks to the mountains and valleys and forests surrounding me it was safe, enclosed, peaceful. And limited. You can see only so far in any direction before the landscape eclipses your view of the distance.

Hiking and mountain climbing are popular hobbies, perhaps lending a different perspective allowing one to see for miles instead. I have friends who are "46ers" – a special group of relentless hikers who have climbed all the high peaks of the Adirondacks, 46 in total, with Mount Marcy capping off the highest of the high peaks.

In Tampa, however, it is flat. You can see sky forever when you look up and the horizon off the bays seem so distant. I realized quickly that I could watch the full sunset from my balcony over the bay every night. At my house in New York, I could see the sky change colors during sundown, but the trees and elevation changes eclipsed the actual sunset. I have watched more sundowners here than ever in my life before!

There is water everywhere, and something very calming in the air that seems to go with the waves and palm trees. While not much of Tampa remains "no shirt, no shoes, no problem," that carefree, come-as-you-are mentality persists. I had to leave my New York at the border and focus on slowing down.

At first this part was tough, and I had to force myself to relax, but over my first year in Tampa I have learned to be more patient. And more friendly. People like to say hello more than in New York, especially when you are out with a cute dog.

Tampa is a very dog-friendly town, and well-behaved pups are welcome on most patios and inside some bars, restaurants, and stores. Lots of businesses leave water out and drinking fountains are designed with a lower catch bowl for our canine friends.

I began walking dogs when I first came to Tampa as a way to make some cash, meet some fun dogs (and people), and learn my way around town. I would be walking for exercise regardless, so I might as well walk with some cool dogs and make a little cash at the same time.

I have some regulars now that I adore – looking at you, Jager, Rambo, Buddy, and Tally – and it has been a great side gig. Having a dog of my own would be a challenge at the moment, so getting to love on other people's pups is perfect!

Side note, this is also my amazing sister's business in North Carolina; she has been successful and exceptionally happy working with dogs for several years. Very much recommend if you love dogs and are looking for a side gig!

27° 56′ 14″ N, 82° 28′ 59″ W

I acutely felt the new orientation of Tampa – 27°N, 82°W – like my body felt different in its place on earth. One of my first purchases to decorate my new apartment was a handcrafted wood sign with the South Tampa coordinates. It *feels* tropical, southern, almost foreign here.

One thing I didn't expect was how much stronger the sun would be here. I mean, I knew it would be hotter of course, and that there would be more of it. But during the midday hours for much of the year, the sun can be excruciating.

One day in the middle of my first February in Tampa I was driving through downtown in the heart of the city, surrounded by beautiful skyscrapers. Heat was radiating off the pavement, stuck in the maze of downtown buildings, and the sun was directly overhead, no clouds in the sky.

It was unbearably hot even with the A/C on max and, sitting at a traffic light, I closed the roof of the Mini for the first time ever because it was too hot – in mid-February! I wondered then what I was in for...

I've been here for a year now and I keep waiting for the 'on-vacation' feeling to wear off and it hasn't yet. There is some cognitive dissonance while waiting for it to get cold or for some noticeable change in season and it's hard to remember to buy Christmas presents. Daylight saving time seemed to come out of nowhere.

I check the weather in New York often. It feels surreal seeing wintertime temperatures up there while I am still in shorts down here. I see pics of snowmen and ski days. New York friends are blanketing their horses and I know how thick Ducky's grey winter coat would be now.

It feels like a distant memory, like time is mismatched and running at different speeds.

Becoming Florida

Relocating is full of huge things and tiny things, all these small details that taken together add up to one human life. Some things were more exciting than others. Switching my auto insurance was not so exciting as it turns out Upstate New York rates are rather reasonable but getting my new Florida driver's license was cool!

Selling my house and e-signing the final documents was an incredible relief but one that set in over time. It did not feel real at first. I still woke up at night worrying about something – a burst pipe, vandalism, storm damage, the obvious vacancy of the house, even weeks after the closing officially made the house someone else's dream. Letting go of it was one huge step toward Becoming Florida.

The day I updated my car registration and picked up my new Endless Summer license plate was a big deal for me! I'm still getting used to cars having only one license plate on the back – in New York you need a front and rear plate, but Florida only requires the rear plate. My

Florida plate looks amazing on my Mini and it inspires me, especially since the climate was a huge reason for my move.

Endless hot, hazy, sunny days and cool bay breezes filtered through the palms and mangroves filled my fantasies and now my reality. Hot summer nights reignite memories of childhood vacations to Disney where the sticky nights overwhelmed my senses.

The license plate features a surfer walking on the beach at sunset; gorgeous imagery and colors that punctuated my tropical dreams for years before moving here.

Some days I wake up and in those murky seconds before opening my eyes when sleep is slowly fading, I feel like I'm still in my old house. The windows are oriented the same in my new bedroom overlooking the bay but that is where the similarities end between the old house and my new apartment. With full consciousness comes the memory of relocating, the reality of living at 82 degrees West.

Each box I check off is one more piece of the New York me falling away. Voter registration, check. Home insurance to renter's, check. New doctor, new bank. Check, check. Swap snow scraper for sunscreen, enthusiastic check on that one!

I still need a few things in Tampa. But the pieces of me that were New York are fading away slowly as I check more boxes. I find myself mixing a little sweet tea in my usual unsweetened at restaurants. Grits are my go-to breakfast side and I secretly love it when my boyfriend grabs my hand and sings along to the local country station in the car.

Not long ago, I made an impulsive purchase, one that I never expected to make but that feels right. A gently used Jimmy Buffet blue and yellow beach cruiser is now my casual transportation – or will be, once I relearn to ride!

A jaunty bright green parrot is the horn and a sweet yellow basket rests in front of the handlebars. Oh, and it has a bottle opener on the frame in case a cool one needs to be opened. It is a beauty!

It will, I am sure, become its own story soon.

One more step in Becoming Florida.

The night of the closing of my New York house, several long weeks after I had settled in Florida, I sat on the balcony listening to the sea birds and bay waves and tree frogs, celebrating the closure of that chapter, and imagining the new family celebrating their fresh start in my old house.

It was a heady realization to think of strangers building new memories in the place I called mine for so long. Letting go, moving forward, celebrating new beginnings and old familiarities.

Leaving New York. Becoming Florida.

Florida Me

I'm different, too. It isn't just the sunsets and vibrant colors and seabirds, it's me, too. I'm happy. I've been thinking a lot about the differences between being happy, like the state of genuinely being content and happy overall, versus happiness in a moment or happiness with a thing. I know I was happy with Ducky, and when traveling, and hanging out with Sasha. But I don't think I was happy in life. I found satisfaction in many things and enjoyed life, for sure. I had fun.

Now, though, I feel happy with life, location, and love. It is overwhelming at times to be driving around this incredible city and catch a surprisingly gorgeous view, all the while smelling salt air and ocean breezes and Mark's hand is on my thigh and the radio is playing Luke Bryan.

I feel like the happiest person, and I have no idea how I got so lucky. I fill my social media posts now with hashtags like #loveyourlife and #luckygirl and #changeyourlife.

I smile at strangers.

And I've started singing along to the country songs, too.

I suffered from seasonal depression in New York for years. I thought it was normal to hibernate in the winter, to never leave the couch, staring outside at barren tree branches silhouetted against grey skies. Dark nights mirrored dark thoughts.

It was hard to make myself do much or take joy in much. But it was my norm to start feeling crappy sometime in early November, to gain weight and lose energy. My skin would be tight and itchy, dry even after moisturizers, and my nails would crack and break. I hated how it hurt to breathe when I went outside, and I dreaded fearing I might slip on ice.

But I never questioned it, whether I had to feel this way or if there was another way to live. I was too deep in my routine and complacent in life to wonder if I were happy or not, or if I could be happier.

Once I started questioning it, though, I couldn't stop. I wanted more sun and less winter. More bright and less drab. More happy, less sad. After living in Tampa for a while and going into my first November when I would normally begin feeling bad, I realized I just... wasn't. I felt good and had more energy than ever. The seasonal depression, my constant cold-weather companion, had left me.

It's easy to forget now as I write this how bad it was before I left. How badly I needed to leave. My body was holding so much tension. I couldn't turn my head in a full rotation in any direction – side to side, up, down, in circles. My neck was too tight, and that tension radiated down my shoulders and back and up into my head.

My best efforts to relax it went unrewarded. The harder I tried, the worse it was. After the move, though, my muscles finally let go. Full range of motion is back, I can move and turn my head and rest comfortably.

When I can't sleep now it's because I am consumed with planning, or sometimes writing stories in my head. In New York, my insomnia was more about panic than purpose. It was wasted energy spent worrying rather than being productive. It was cold nights spent alone.

It was wanting change but not making change happen, wishing for a different reality I was too afraid to dream of, too scared to try.

Leaping in and moving and leaving my job and my past taught me to dream big and make things happen for myself. Taking control, making myself happy.

I have long wondered how much place defines person. In my case, I've come to realize it matters a lot.

I may not be Abi in New York with MetLife now and that's okay with me. I am more me than ever, becoming Florida me, the new me. Who I was meant to be, leaving the old me behind with my wool sweaters and down parkas and business cards in MetLife blue.

Chapter 10 – Grateful

Truth is, we can't do it all ourselves. This last year proved that to me, even if I want to think I can do everything alone. There is a certain comfort in this, though. Letting down defenses, lowering walls. Even I can do that from time to time.

Over my life I have built up defenses, like we all have, to protect myself. I hate being made fun of, and as I have reflected it was something that grew up over my childhood always feeling like I had to be on edge to survive.

A former work mentor asked me once why I thought the world was out to get me, which was very insightful. At the time I did not have a great answer, but I knew I had been trying to keep myself safe and it was a learned habit over my lifetime.

Letting go of that safety defense, learning to trust others and accept help from others and be grateful for that help, that was another huge leap.

Thanks, B.

I mentioned B. and the U-Haul unit earlier in this book, but he deserves his own section here. I am forever grateful because he taught me to accept help – a first in getting comfortable being uncomfortable. This is the story in more detail.

I rented a storage unit at U-Haul to use as I was cleaning out my house, staging it, and prepping for sale. It was conveniently right down the road from my house. But... have you ever moved houses using a Mini Cooper convertible? It takes a while. Often when I was taking a load of boxes back to my unit, I would see B.

He worked at U-Haul and had rented me my unit. He was young, nice, and ambitious. We talked about Tampa, and he had lived there before and told me how much I would love it. Sometimes we waved to each other across the parking lot. It was nice to have a friendly face there.

B. watched me make countless trips with the Mini. Maybe he watched over me. One night I told him I was planning to move my things out over the next few weeks and relinquish the storage unit. It was going to take as many trips to move out as it did in, around 30.

Have you been inside a storage unit facility? It is a bit of a maze of aisles and units. The lights were on motion detectors and sometimes the bulbs burned out. The doors to units were usually locked but some were not, and they would sporadically swing open when you passed. This facility had a second level and to access those units there were huge ladders on wheels. Their portability meant you could walk around a corner and into a ladder without warning.

It was a creepy place on its own merit, added to it the potential creepiness of other people who rented units and might be inside, too... I only had one encounter with someone inside the facility that I would have rather not met. My intuition kicked into high gear when

I walked past that person, and I was grateful it was on my way out. But knowing B. kept an eye on me made me feel safer.

When I told him I was moving out of the unit, B. told me he would have a truck the next evening after work and would help me move my stuff back to my house. I was flabbergasted! Why would this almost-stranger help me move in the cold November night?

It's hard enough to convince friends and people who love you to help you move, let alone a stranger who has worked all day. He pushed aside my objections and I gratefully accepted, the image of myself moving 30 carloads of boxes alone back to my house swirling in my head.

The next night, we met at U-Haul and loaded my things into the back of his rented truck. He followed me to my house and unloaded the U-Haul. When we were finished, we chatted for a minute, then he left. This kind, sweet man had helped me for no reason other than to be helpful when I needed it.

I teared up watching the U-Haul leave. Spending a cold night helping a stranger move was more kindness than I could imagine someone extending me. Honestly, I couldn't imagine doing that for someone else before that night.

In the months since, I have thought about B. and that night often. I still can't exactly explain it. He showed up in my life at the right time, and his gentle, calm personality meant he was able to slide under my usual defenses effortlessly.

I have long prided myself on my independence and this last year has humbled me in that regard. Having to accept help, ask for help, even, was not in my comfort zone. I didn't know how to do it. I was too used to protecting myself, staying isolated in myself and my house and my comfortable life.

Reaching out, admitting to someone else that I needed help when I couldn't even admit it to myself was too much for me. Yet there we were, two almost-strangers working side by side in the night.

I still struggle with asking for help and admitting I can't do it all myself. And I am grateful to have learned more about kindness that night. Thank you, B.

My HillCroft Family

The time I spent at HillCroft changed me. That is not a sentence I type lightly; there are very few things I can look back at and say absolutely changed who I am and the course of my life. My trainers, Sally and Karol, and Karol's daughter Kelley, gave me life, direction, and laughs.

And Ducky. I am forever grateful for the time with her, and to them for sharing her with me.

My life is better because of these women. They taught me centered riding and to center myself. I learned grace, balance, and compassion in my time there.

It's interesting, we don't often realize these moments are incredible when we experience them. Sometimes it's obvious, like when you finally try a long-anticipated restaurant and order your favorite dish or go on a bucket list trip to a meaningful place.

We know in the moment these times are amazing and maybe we focus on enjoying them more because we recognize that. But what about the everyday times? The little moments that maybe we don't realize right away are adding up to a favorite memory.

Things like when I was tacking up Duck and it was time for her bridle – I would unhook the crossties, put the reins over her neck, and unclip her halter. She would smirk and throw her face to the sky stretching her neck. At 17.1 hands, she quickly bested me with height, so I would just laugh and scratch her neck.

She would tease me, lowering her face to me to allow a quick muzzle rub but raising it if I moved the bridle toward her, her amusement visible in her innocent eyes. This was one of her favorite games and it was not anything I could rush. She was in control of this one, a total mare move. Once she was ready, though, she lowered her face into my arms and gently took the bit.

I spent hours there, it just happens at a horse barn. It's called barn time, and the struggle is real. Some of my best times were spent sitting in the indoor ring with friends, watching lessons and learning, a barn cat curled up in my lap, Ducky quietly napping in her stall, sunlight streaming into the arena, the smell of fresh hay and oiled leather in the air, the soft drum of hoofbeats and nickers from the horses in the barn. Sally would always ask about my love life and Karol would give me a hug and tell me I looked great.

So many of these little moments at the barn, repeating themselves daily at horse farms across the world. It's an amazing world.

Showing Gratitude

There are lots of ways people show gratitude, like saying thanks or I love you or doing something for someone else. Perhaps you have heard about Oprah's gratitude journal where she instructs you to write down three things every day that you are grateful for.

Maybe they are big things, like having a safe place to live and the ability to feed your children.

Maybe they are little things, like your partner bringing you coffee or your kitten purring in your lap, making all the green lights, hearing the birds sing, watching the sun rise over the horizon.

Maybe reading these few examples made you smile and feel a rush of happiness or gratefulness. I can see where Oprah is coming from. This works.

But I learned by leaping in – there is so much more. I can find gratitude in unexpected places. It is how you look at things. A seemingly negative situation may have more positives than you first imagine and finding them can make you happy. It is the same idea as choosing happiness. If there is a remedy available that would work, why not try it and be happy?

Mark sometimes snores at night (I mean, me too, we're all human). We laugh at the sleep app recordings but occasionally, when combined with my frequent bouts of insomnia, it keeps me up at night. When that happens, I leave the bedroom and work in the office or go in the guest bedroom with Sash.

I could stay in bed, tossing and turning and getting annoyed, growing resentment like a thorny wall between us, maybe waking him, too, and neither of us would sleep well. Or I could choose happiness and find a remedy, like going to the other bedroom.

This simple act of choosing to make change, even a tiny one like sleeping in the guest room, is liberating. Taking action where before you were inert can set off an amazing domino effect of great things. Remember the LEAP Model – taking action is an important step.

Chapter 11 – Relocation is a Leap

Leaping in is a personality trait. The last year has been full of huge leaps for me – getting laid off; moving across the country; selling my first house; renting my first apartment in 15 years; starting my first company; and falling in love. I joked that I was going to do all the big life changes at once – comedy as stress-relief. But when I look back throughout my life, leaping in has been my lifestyle.

I love the thrill of immersing myself in a new hobby or idea – reading a book in one weekend or obsessively studying a new concept until I get it right. It is finding the perfect chocolate cake recipe and recreating it at home until I can make it in my sleep (try adding espresso!).

It is falling in love with a place I've only read about until I can visit time after time, memorizing the way the cobblestones rise toward the canals and where my favorite graffiti is and how the old church stone feels smooth and cold under my fingertips. It is collecting every hardcover ever published by my favorite author and obsessively reading their beautiful prose over and over.

Leaping in is who I am.

Maybe the most important thing I have learned is to be unafraid of what others think. So many people will tell you it isn't possible, you can't do it, don't try it. This is utter nonsense. What they are actually saying is it is not possible for them, they cannot do it, they did not try it. It has nothing to do with your ability to be successful; rather it is about them and their lack of success. Truly, screw those people. Their fear does not hold you back.

You are enough. Be excited about what you are doing. It will be hard because some of the people telling you not to try will be people you love. Lots of people can only see one way of doing things so deviation from that worries them.

Fear is a powerful motivator for some. Change is a powerful motivator for others. The amazing thing is you get to pick – fear or change. Which one motivates you?

Leap of Faith

Is that what this last year was? In a way, leaping in could be called a leap of faith. You have no guarantee for how things will turn out on the other side of your leap. Believing in the change continuum means either outcome will be positive, but the initial step into the dark abyss is terrifying. Maybe that is why I leap – I have always been a jump-in-the-pool person.

To me, a leap of faith implies trying something that feels huge – and doing it with nothing more than hope for a good outcome. That's incredibly brave when you think about it.

Lessons Learned

I have learned nostalgic does not equal sad. That Florida and New York are both incredible places. That I need the sun, and a simple change in latitude changes everything. A literal new view triggers new points of view, new ideas, and new thoughts.

I am still me, but I am becoming Florida me. The Florida me is more relaxed, more sun-kissed, and she is way happier.

I learned I can't go back. For a long time, my fantasy was buying back my childhood home in Rhinebeck and hosting elaborate holidays and summertime pool parties - those things I loved as a child growing up in our drafty Victorian.

I realized somewhere along the way that it wouldn't work, though. Even if I could go back to our familial house, I couldn't go back to feeling the way I did as the girl living in our yellow house on Mill Street. I'm not her anymore.

I used to see the past in a very rosy way – I loved my hometown and house and horse. And that is where it ended. The small town was, in my eyes, beautiful, liberal, smart. I didn't see everything, though. Like a child does, I saw Rhinebeck in its idealistic glory, the uglier parts kept swept to the side from the curious eyes of children.

As an adult, I still love my hometown – walking down East Market Street and passing the familiar shops takes me back to sidewalk sales in the 80s with my mom and sister.

I can't go to Rhinebeck without stepping into the past at Stickle's, the old-time five-and-dime that smells the same as it did when I was little buying posterboard for my prize-winning seventh-grade science fair project. Winter Sun (and its companion store, Summer Moon) captured my awe as a teen with their display of handcrafted leather bags, brightly colored clothes, and silver rings popping out of baskets of rice by the cash register.

An alternative bookstore opened in town when I was a teen, Oblong Books. I spent many happy hours there browsing for books to suit my changing interests and teenaged convictions. The candy shop in town is now owned by some very famous Hollywood types.

But when Ira started it, I was in high school, struggling to fit in and stand out at the same time, to find a place I could be me. He became a mentor of sorts to many kids. Adults like Ira who understand kids and provide a safe place to be are priceless.

I've learned all places have flaws. It is whether we choose to see them or not. Seeing opportunity instead of failure, good instead of bad. So many things in life are what we make them; what we choose to make them. Now I choose positivity, happiness, beauty.

Am I still leaping in?

I am finally happy. One year later, and a lifetime leading up to now, and I am finally happy. Leaping into new places, new people, and new projects has energized me. For once, maybe for the first time, I am excited for the future, and excited to see what happens tomorrow.

Sometimes Mark makes me laugh so hard I can't think, or we go somewhere so incredibly beautiful and I'm overwhelmed with emotions. Whitney Houston said it better than me when she sang "I fall in love whenever we meet" and yes, exactly this! It is true of my city, my boyfriend, and now, my life. I fall in love with me every day.

I am practicing mindfulness and gratefulness daily now, and still leaping in.

All the changes of the last year are just my most recent leap, but they will not be my last.

Leaping in is a personality trait, a love affair with life. It is eating dessert first and kissing someone you love and riding the horse that gives you chills and traveling to incredible corners of the world where your breath catches in your throat at the beauty of it all.

Diving into the deep end, feeling alive, and finding yourself through change. Living, loving, leaping every day.

Live well, embrace change, and leap in.

***

Thank you

There are many people to whom I'm grateful for their help in getting this book out of my head and into your hands. You'll recognize some of them from the stories in this book.

A big thanks to my editor, Debbie, and book mentor, Amy W. – your advice and guidance helped immeasurably. Amy, thanks also for your push at breakfast – who knew a quick Tweet over French Toast in Siesta Key would be the confidence boost I needed to publish this work!

Special thanks to the many friends who offered a supportive word and lent an ear as I leapt into writing this book – Mike K., Gregg G., and Rob G. in particular.

Katryn, thank you for your beautiful nature and generous friendship, and for establishing a place where people can thrive, be themselves, and be creative.

To my HillCroft Family, and especially Karol, Sally, and Kelley – thank you for Ducky. She is part of my soul and will forever be the most elegant and free-spirited piece of me. She lives in my dreams and my favorite memories.

To Dan, who has lived his life exemplifying the meaning of leaping in, thank you for your friendship and undying belief in me. From Hawaii to Zurich, your confidence in me made me leap further than ever. Cigars, Swiss Alps, and fondue with you will always be my favorite vacation memory!

Thank you to my parents for instilling a love of reading in me. There were many years when a Dean Koontz hardcover was my prized Christmas gift. My love for words has long been a motivating force in my life. Watching my dad devour a stack of books has always inspired me and knowing he reads my words now is one of the most incredible things in my life.

Thank you to my sister, Melissa, for your support over the years and in the writing of this book. No one else knows my story quite the same way and still loves me after it all!

I owe the world to Ramya, Elaine, and Denise – your grace, support, confidence, beauty, compassion, and drive inspire me every day to be a better woman – thank you a million times!

And to Mark. You make me better and I can't imagine doing this without you. Thanks for always believing in me and making me believe in myself. Thank you for being my partner and going through this life with me. You're amazing and neat. Love you.

***

About the Author

Abi is an author, traveler, and lover of life. She lives in South Tampa with her cat, Sasha. Connect with her at www.LifeAfterLeapingIn.com.

The author at home in New York. Photo courtesy of the author.

Also Written by Abi Potter Clough

Top 10 Lists For Relocation

Please Write a Review

I'd love to hear your thoughts on *Life After Leaping In*! Please leave me a review on Amazon.